REACHES
OF HEAVEN

OTHER BOOKS BY
ISAAC BASHEVIS SINGER

NOVELS

THE MANOR

I. THE MANOR   II. THE ESTATE

THE FAMILY MOSKAT   THE MAGICIAN OF LUBLIN

SATAN IN GORAY   THE SLAVE

ENEMIES, A LOVE STORY

SHOSHA

STORIES

A FRIEND OF KAFKA   GIMPEL THE FOOL   SHORT FRIDAY

THE SÉANCE   THE SPINOZA OF MARKET STREET

A CROWN OF FEATHERS   PASSIONS   OLD LOVE

MEMOIRS

IN MY FATHER'S COURT

FOR CHILDREN

A DAY OF PLEASURE   THE FOOLS OF CHELM

MAZEL AND SHLIMAZEL OR THE MILK OF A LIONESS

WHEN SHLEMIEL WENT TO WARSAW   A TALE OF THREE WISHES

ELIJAH THE SLAVE   JOSEPH AND KOZA OR THE SACRIFICE TO THE VISTULA

ALONE IN THE WILD FOREST   THE WICKED CITY

NAFTALI THE STORYTELLER AND HIS HORSE, SUS

WHY NOAH CHOSE THE DOVE

COLLECTION

AN ISAAC BASHEVIS SINGER READER

Isaac Bashevis Singer

REACHES OF HEAVEN

A STORY OF THE BAAL SHEM TOV

With twenty-three original etchings by

IRA MOSKOWITZ

FARRAR · STRAUS · GIROUX / NEW YORK

Text copyright © 1980 by Isaac Bashevis Singer
Illustrations copyright © 1980 by Ira Moskowitz
First printing, 1980
Printed in the United States of America
Published simultaneously in Canada by McGraw-Hill Ryerson Ltd., Toronto

Library of Congress Cataloging in Publication Data
Singer, Isaac Bashevis.
Reaches of heaven.
1. Israel ben Eliezer, Baal Shem Tov, called
BeSHT, 1700 (ca.)–1760 — Fiction. I. Moskowitz, Ira.
II. Title.
PZ3.S61657   Re 1980   [PJ5129.S49]   839'.0933
ISBN 0-374-24733-1   80-36672

A limited deluxe first edition of this book in 275 copies
has been privately printed by Landmark Press

This short book does not pretend to be a biography of Rabbi Israel Baal Shem Tov by any means. So little is known about his life that no life story is possible. This work is nothing more than the writer's impressions or fantasies of Rabbi Israel's way of thinking, his emotions, his spiritual achievements and disappointments. The few "miracles" told here are all ambiguous and could easily be explained in a psychological way. I see Rabbi Israel as a man of deep belief in God and of much doubt in man and his abilities to reach perfection. He was, like all great religious thinkers, a lonely man, both primitive and refined, enchanted by the divine powers and pained by man's suffering, by his bitter struggle and often by his pettiness.

The Baal Shem Tov did not write any books and that which is being said or told in his name is often of dubious value. But his spirit is frequently expressed in the works and stories of his great-grandson Rabbi Nachman of Bratslav, one of the greatest religious minds of all times. I.B.S.

ILLUSTRATIONS

REACHES
OF HEAVEN

I

THE VILLAGE OF OKUP, on the border of Volhynia, was small and old. For several decades it had been under Turkish rule, and then it was occupied by the Poles. By the time the Poles entered Okup, the kingdoms of both Turkey and Poland had lost their former importance. The Turks had exhausted their might in incessant wars. Poland was about to disintegrate because each squire was like a king on his estate, often with his own army and his own laws.

The Jews had been in exile some 1700 years, had wandered from land to land and had spoken God knows how many languages. But they had not forgotten their Holy Land, their God and their sacred books. This world was nothing but a narrow corridor for them—a ghetto that led to the mansions of Paradise and to the days of the Messiah. The purpose of life was Torah and good deeds.

Among the residents of Okup at the time of the Polish takeover was a pious Jew by the name of Eliezer who had been held a prisoner by the Turks for many years. Reb Eliezer was known as a scholar and a cabbalist. It is told that a holy man had promised Reb Eliezer that his wife would give birth to a son who would be a Light of the Exile. Reb Eliezer's son was born in the year 1700 and was given the name Israel. He had white skin, blue eyes and blond hair.

Israel soon became an orphan, for both Reb Eliezer and his wife passed away at an early age. After the death of his parents, the boy slept in an orphanage and "ate days," which meant that he got his meals every day of the week in a different house.

The Jewish community of Okup, like that of all other towns and villages with sizeable Jewish populations, did not allow its orphans to grow up untutored. Young Israel was sent to a cheder, where he learned to read Hebrew, studied the Pentateuch with Rashi commentary and soon began to study the Gemara. It was quickly realized that he had a mind well suited to scholarly pursuits.

In cheder Israel was known as a storyteller. Some of the stories he had heard from others—old men, old women, wandering beggars—and some he invented himself. The tales dealt with cabbalists who could tap wine from a wall and create live pigeons through the power of holy names; with angels who revealed themselves to mystics and divulged to them the secrets of the cabbala; as well as with wild squires, sorcerers, demons, imps and hobgoblins. The powers of good and the powers of evil waged an eternal war. On one side there were God, the angels, pious Jews, the Torah and the infinite worlds which the servants of God were to inherit. On the other side were Satan, Asmodeus, Lilith, Naamah, Machlath, as well as multitudes of pagans, murderers, lechers, harlots, whose purpose was to extinguish the light of the Godhead and to establish the dominion of wickedness forever. From Cain, Balaam, Pharaoh the King of Egypt, Amalek, the wicked Haman, the hetman Bogdan Chmielnicki followed a long chain of murder, lechery, defilement, idolatry. One could not deny that the Evil One also managed to lure quite a number of Jews into the desire to exchange the world to come for the precarious pleasures of this world—Jews like Jeroboam, the son of Nebat; Elisha, the son of Abihu; and the false messiah Sabbatai Zvi.

Sabbatai Zvi, who lived only about a hundred years before the boy Israel was born, promised the Jews that he would bring the redemption, but when the Sultan imprisoned him in a fortress, he put on the fez of a Mohammedan and changed his faith. Remnants of Sabbatai Zvi's followers still lived in Turkish lands and were called Donmas. Every Friday they went out to the fields expecting Sabbatai Zvi to descend from Heaven riding on a donkey and to bring the End of Days. They believed that the one who had converted was not Sabbatai Zvi himself, but his shadow. The real Sabbatai Zvi had ascended to a Heavenly mansion called the Bird's Nest and dwelled there together with such angels and seraphim as Metatron—the Lord of the Face—Sandalfon and Gabriel. There were also some clandestine prophets of Sabbatai Zvi among the Jews in Poland, Bohemia, Germany and other countries. They preached to their disciples that the Messiah would come to the Jews only when the whole generation would

be guilty, immersed in iniquity. Not good deeds, but transgressions and abominations would bring salvation. Some of those satanic leaders secretly wrote talismans with the names of Sabbatai Zvi and his pupils, Nathan of Gaza and Samuel Primo, as well as the names of devils, vampires and evil spirits of all kinds. They maintained that God and Satan must ultimately join together because both of them are actually the same.

The prodigy Israel from the village of Okup pondered these matters, and he soon decided to stand on the side of the holy powers that were bound to bring the true Messiah.

II

THE BOYS IN CHEDER played all kinds of games: hide-and-seek, tag, goat and wolf; on Chanukah, it was spin the dreidel and even cards. But young Israel, or Srulik as his friends called him, had no patience for games. He thought a grownup's thoughts. Surreptitiously, he perused philosophical tracts and volumes of the cabbala. He was fully aware that one dared not study the cabbala before the age of thirty, since this could lead to heresy or even madness, but he couldn't wait that long.

Countless questions assailed his brain, and he had to find answers for them. In the credo he recited each weekday after morning prayers, it said that God had existed forever, that He wasn't corporeal and therefore was not to be perceived by those who employed material concepts. But how was it possible to exist forever? How could there be a being who hadn't a beginning? What had God done in all the time prior to His creation of the world?

In Genesis it is written that, with the power of His word, God had created the heaven and the earth, the oceans, the sun, the moon, the stars, all the beasts and Adam and Eve. But how could a word form a person, a lion, a river, a stone? And since God was omnipotent, why did He allow the idolaters to dominate all the lands and let the Jews, the people He had chosen from all the nations, suffer for almost two millennia in exile? True, the Jews had sinned, and God punished them, but hadn't the gentiles sinned even more? Srulik had heard many stories about Bogdan Chmielnicki's times and of the savageries the Cossacks had perpetrated upon saintly Jews, pious Jewesses and in-

nocent children. How could a merciful God observe such cruelties and remain silent?

The older Srulik grew and the more he pondered, the more obvious it became to him that he wouldn't find complete answers in the Bible, in the Talmud or even in the volumes of the philosophers—in *Guide for the Perplexed*, in *Khuzari*, in *Faiths and Opinions*. Only the cabbala devoted itself to the secrets of heaven and earth. True, it was dangerous to probe such volumes when one was still young, but the boy from Okup was ready to risk body and soul to find answers to his questions.

In the attic above the studyhouse in Okup reposed old sacred books with yellowed pages, bound in wooden covers or lacking covers altogether and overlain with dust. Israel had heard it said that, some generations earlier, a wicked ruler had issued an edict to burn all religious books, and the Jews had therefore hidden them away in the attic. Within the years, most of the books had been eaten by moths and many had been water-soaked by the rains that poured through the holey roof. The presiding rabbi then decreed that the torn books should be left undisturbed and that the community should buy new ones, since young lads who were taught from mutilated and dusty volumes lost the urge to study. The older people, on the other hand, no longer had sharp vision and were liable to go blind, God forbid, trying to decipher moldy tomes with letters that were half obliterated.

Israel had heard another reason why the books had been left lying in the attic. During the time of the false messiah Sabbatai Zvi, the Jews of Okup had gone astray on the teachings of the false messiah. Some local scholars had inscribed praises to Sabbatai Zvi on the margins of the sacred books; others had even tried to alter the texts and to excise passages that didn't agree with their beliefs. Following the end of the Sabbatai Zvi nightmare, the Jews didn't want the younger generation to study from volumes desecrated by the false messiah's disciples.

However, Srulik wasn't frightened off by all these dangers. He had found up in the attic such cabbala volumes as *The Book of Creation, The Orchard of Pomegranates* by Rabbi Moses of Cordoba, *The Tree of Life* by Rabbi Isaac Luria, as well as cabbala manuscripts that had never been printed and had remained in handwritten form. Srulik was too young to understand the various versions of the cabbala, but he gathered its essence—that the world was a part of God. God's light was concealed in every rock, every creature, every plant. Even the peasants in the marketplace and the drunkards in the taverns were formed of divine substance.

Gradually, through the course of emanations, out of concealment and revelation, out of enveloping light and shadow, did spirit become matter. According to the cabbala, the World of Deeds, our Earth, was the lowest of all the worlds God had created. Down here, on Earth, light was transformed into stone, bone, mountains, valleys.

It can be said that the Earth is a mask of God which appears in many contradictions —good and evil, refined and coarse, alive and dead, enduring and transitory. But behind this cover of plurality is hidden God's oneness. The boulder and the soap bubble are identical. Stupidity is only crippled wisdom. The dead aren't dead, the departed haven't vanished. God lives, and everything that comes from Him is alive. Darkness is only dimmed light. The wrongs are disguised mercies.

Why did God require this concealment? asks the cabbala. And its answer is: God bestowed upon the people of the Earth—which is the lowest and darkest of all the worlds —a gift that no other world could have received: free will, the freedom to choose between good and evil. In the higher spheres, God's light is too radiant to allow doubt and error. The angels, seraphim, cherubim and aralim all love God, acknowledge His wisdom, His beauty, His goodness. Up there, there can be no thieves, murderers, liars, lechers. There are, indeed, various degrees of spirituality in these higher worlds, but even the least of them yearns to serve God, to enjoy His splendor. Only down here on Earth does Satan have almost as much dominion as God, and sometimes he has even more. Down here, man must constantly choose between justice and injustice, between the path which leads to the realms of exaltation and that which leads to the netherworld.

In a sense, man is his own master. So long as he breathes, he can either build or destroy. In the chain of creation, man is the weakest link. If man uplifts himself spiritually, does good, helps others, he can fortify the whole chain of creation. If he defiles and weakens his own link, he endangers God's divine scheme.

The cabbala volumes young Srulik read didn't supply the answer to *all* of the boy's questions. In his later years, Israel realized that the questions and doubts of the human brain cannot be answered so long as the soul reposes within the body. But plunging into the cabbala books raised his spirit. He, Israel son of Eliezer, was no longer an orphan in the small town of Okup, but a part of God, a link in the chain of world creation. Angels and high spirits waited for him to behave as God had commanded, to help the sacred powers overcome the forces of debasement and thus speed redemption.

III

THE TIME FLEW. One day Srulik was a boy, and then, almost overnight, he was a young man. Imbued with a fear of God, he left cheder and went to the yeshiva to pursue a life of scholarship. Most of the youths hurried through their prayers, but Israel prayed slowly. Some of the prayers he chanted in melodies he himself composed.

Although he was nothing more than a poor youth who still depended on charity for his support, he was accorded respect by the inhabitants of his town. His face was remarkably pure, and his eyes reflected the joy of one who has found gratification in knowledge.

The youth developed a mode of life suited to his meditative disposition. He went to bed early and rose with the sun. In the summers, he took long walks through the fields and woods around Okup. He never tired of seeing the sun rise each morning fresh and renewed, washed clean in the heavenly oceans. He listened to the twittering of the birds. Even the lowing of the cows and the whinnying of the horses exalted his spirit. Since the world was divine, he could find God in every tree, every flower, every blade of grass, every butterfly. The world rejoiced in being a world. How could the Earth be dead if it gave birth to life?

A stream ran through the forest of Okup, and Israel would immerse himself in it before donning his phylacteries and reciting his morning prayers. Afterwards, he would savor a slice of bread that he had brought along for his breakfast. Some of the yeshiva students hurried through their meals, gulped down the food unchewed. They complained that the dishes served them were tasteless. But all this was due to their hurry. Whoever is confident that God has created every stalk of rye and every drop of water, tastes the flavor of Paradise in everything he eats or drinks.

On Tuesdays, Israel always took his meals at the home of a once rich man, Reb Shlomo Tereshpoler. Reb Shlomo had run an inn for a squire but had lost his lease to a Jewish competitor. When Israel had heard that someone had usurped Reb Shlomo's inn, he had been overwhelmed with grief, for Reb Shlomo was an honest, charitable and scholarly man. At the time, Israel had felt that he should stop taking meals at Reb Shlomo's house, for he was reluctant to take charity from a poor man. He had confided this thought to the head of his yeshiva, who advised him against doing so, since it would have humiliated Reb Shlomo. Israel was grateful for this piece of advice, for he enjoyed the members of Reb Shlomo's household, his collection of books and the graciousness with which he was received by his family. Reb Shlomo had a tall, dark-haired son, Abraham Gershon. Abraham Gershon and Israel were close friends. The boys had studied together in cheder and later attended the same yeshiva. Reb Shlomo also had a younger daughter, Ittele. Israel was often so preoccupied by his conversation with Abraham Gershon that he would forget to eat, and Ittele would keep reminding him that his groats were getting cold.

Although in those days people married young in the Jewish towns, and Ittele was already fifteen, she wasn't yet betrothed. The reason for this was that Reb Shlomo no longer had sufficient money to provide a dowry for her, to give the groom the customary presents or to make a wedding.

Israel had noticed—even though a youth was not allowed to look at girls—that Ittele was a quiet, modest maiden and beautiful. She had black hair and black eyes, and it occurred to him that she resembled Shulamith of the Song of Songs. True, according to the interpretations of the Gemara and the Midrash, Shulamith symbolized the children of Israel, and her love was the community of Israel's love of God. However, it is also true that the simplest explanation remains valid.

The Evil Spirit, which had been created to place all kinds of temptations before Jews, gave Israel scant rest. He tortured him with desires for the flesh. Sometimes when Israel strolled through the fields he heard the singing of peasant women. Okup was located not far from the Carpathian Mountains, and the yodeling of gentile women and shepherds echoed through the mountains and aroused in Israel a longing that couldn't have

issued from a pure source. One time, when Israel was immersing himself in the forest stream, a naked female emerged from the shrubs at the riverbank. Before the youth realized what he was seeing, he had glimpsed a dazzling female face, loosened hair and breasts. Israel started to run away. He stumbled against rocks and treeroots in the shallow water. He nearly fell and came close to drowning. As he ran, he heard the woman's wanton laughter. He heard a splashing behind him as if the forest female were swimming after him. When Israel finally emerged from the stream, his clothes had vanished. Had the woman taken them? He recalled the story in the Pentateuch of Joseph and Potiphar's wife. Israel began to pray to God to shield him from temptation. He closed his eyes as he murmured the prayers, and when he opened them again, he saw his clothes. The naked female had vanished, and Israel was convinced that she hadn't been human but one of the demons Satan sent out to snare yeshiva students into the net of adultery.

Often, against his will, Israel thought of Ittele. Sometimes his thoughts about her assailed him during prayers or during study. In his imagination he saw himself betrothed to her, standing with her under the wedding canopy and having children with her. Sometimes these fantasies went even further. Israel struggled against them. Why surrender to the vanities of the body when one could contemplate the Creator, love Him and join with Him? But as much as Israel tried to drive these thoughts away, they came back again and again. At the same time, Israel was afraid lest the matchmakers and community elders, who were his providers, force him to become betrothed to some other girl, possibly the daughter of some rude man who could afford to buy a son-in-law by providing a big dowry and costly wedding presents.

On the other hand, Israel knew that everything occurred according to the dictates of Heaven. Forty days before a child is born, it is proclaimed in Heaven, "The daughter of that man shall be joined to the son of that man. . . ."

That which Israel had feared did happen. The matchmakers besieged him with matches. One of the community elders, actually the same one who had acquired Reb Shlomo's inn, proposed to marry off his daughter to Israel. He promised Israel a dowry of six hundred gulden and ten-years' board as well as a gold watch, five volumes of the Pentateuch, a set of the Mishnah, a set of the Talmud bound in leather, a fur-trimmed hat with thirteen points for the Sabbath and two coats, one for summer and another for winter.

Israel knew full well that he was in no position to oppose the will of the community elders who had raised him, paid his tuition, clothed and shod him. Although Israel realized that everything is predetermined, still he prayed inside to become betrothed to the one for whom his heart yearned. Sometimes prayer can negate a divine verdict.

One day as Israel sat in the studyhouse bent over his Talmudic volume, the door opened to admit a man with the raiment of a peasant. He wore a short gabardine, rough cowhide boots and a sheepskin cap despite the heat. In one hand he held a whip; in the other, a sack. His face was tanned from the sun. He strode to the lectern at which Israel sat and in a loud country voice, asked: "Are you the student Israel son of Eliezer, the orphan?"

"Yes, that's me."

"I'm from the village of Grabica. I live there alone, one Jewish family among two hundred peasants. I have three daughters and two sons, one eleven, the other twelve. I kept a tutor for the boys, but he left me in the middle of the term and went home. It seems, he missed his wife. The oldest boy is to become bar mitzvah within a year, and I want him to learn the weekly portion of the Torah and all the rest. I've been told you're skilled in studies and that's why. . . ."

The country Jew, Haskell, proposed to feed Israel, give him a place to sleep and pay him a fee of four gulden for the term. This would be the first time since Israel had been orphaned that he would be earning his own bread, and he quickly accepted. However, his main reason might have been that in the village of Grabica the matchmakers would leave him alone, and he could avoid becoming betrothed to some girl other than Ittele. The country Jew apparently reckoned that the young student would haggle with him about the fee or ask about the food he would be served, but it wasn't Israel's way to concern himself with such trifles.

Only one thing alarmed Israel: maybe the whole offer was the work of Satan? Israel had realized some time before that the Evil Spirit never leaves anyone alone. He constantly finds new ways to snare the weak into the trap of passion, melancholy or heresy. He lurks over man day and night. If he can't persuade someone to sin by day, he sends sinful dreams to pollute his brain with carnal lust at night.

Israel went to tell the rabbi who was head of the yeshiva that he was leaving to become a teacher, and the rabbi tried to dissuade him from going. In a village, there weren't enough holy volumes to properly conduct Jewish studies; nor could one pray there in a quorum, a minyan, the rabbi argued. "Better remain in town and become betrothed," the rabbi said. "I hear you're being offered some lucrative matches. Wasting time in a

village isn't for someone of your stature." But somehow Israel could not follow this advice. After much pondering, he went to say goodbye to Reb Shlomo. Ittele opened the door for Israel and told him that Reb Shlomo was not at home. Israel wasn't accustomed to speaking with girls. During the days he had taken his meals at the house, Ittele had occasionally urged him to eat while the food was still hot or asked him if what he was eating pleased him. At those times Israel would drop his eyes and mumble, "Yes, thank you. It doesn't matter." He well recalled what the books of morals said: looking at a female and talking to her lead to idle chit-chat, which is but one step away from promiscuity. Well, but now he had to talk to Ittele and tell her not to prepare any more meals for him, since he was leaving to become a tutor in Grabica. Israel asked her to convey his thanks to her parents. The truth is that he should also have thanked her for serving him at the table. Ittele had mentioned several times that it was she who cooked for him and shopped for his meals. Ittele and her mother even did his laundry and darned his socks. But Israel was so shy that the words stuck in his throat.

When Ittele heard him say that he was leaving Okup, she emitted something like a sigh, and she seemed temporarily tongue-tied. Then Israel heard her say: "Why are you going away? What will you do all alone in a hamlet like that? We've already gotten used to you here. To us, you are like a member of the family. Once Mama said that you are like a son to her. Those were her very words. I myself am somehow. . . ." Ittele stopped in mid-sentence. She blushed furiously, and even though Israel looked away, he did notice it. They stood opposite one another, silenced by shame. Afterwards, Israel gathered his courage and said: "I won't stay there for long. I'll be coming back shortly, God willing, and. . . ." More he couldn't say.

At that moment the door opened and Abraham Gershon, Ittele's older brother who was betrothed to the Kitewa Rabbi's daughter, came in. Like Israel, Abraham Gershon secretly probed the cabbala. Abraham Gershon was a prodigy who was versed in the Talmud and in Responsa, but when it came to the cabbala, Israel was the more expert. He had a sense of the concealed, and he grasped things that Abraham Gershon didn't understand from the very onset. From time to time both youths would take long walks through fields and gardens, where they spent hours in discussion about the higher spheres. Although Abraham Gershon was older than Israel, he often spoke to Israel as if Israel were the rabbi and he, Abraham Gershon, were his pupil.

IV

IN THE MONTHS Israel stayed in Grabica, he truly grew up. He began to sprout a blond beard. He had parts of days and whole nights to think and read by himself, since Haskell's boys had no urge to study. They raised pigeons, they palled around with gentiles, they actually didn't even know how to pray. Haskell himself was ignorant. Well, but he had compassion for the poor and sick. Nearly all the wandering beggars heading for Okup and the surrounding towns passed through Grabica, and Haskell and his wife, Dvosha, fed them, put them up for the night in their barn and gave them provisions for the road.

Israel devoted himself to the paupers, too. They all had stories to tell—stories of savage landowners, of highwaymen who lurked along the roads, of witches who turned into werewolves or vampires or who rode off on Sabbath eves on brooms to desolate forests to conduct black masses, to eat limbs plucked from live animals, to drink blood and to give themselves over to the devil.

Nor was there any dearth of stories about Jews. Here and there secret disciples of Sabbatai Zvi were unmasked. They still believed that the Messiah could be brought through depravity. Some of them were ritual slaughterers, and they slaughtered cattle and fowl with knives that were blemished so that people would eat impure meat. Surreptitiously, they introduced tallow or milk into meat soup so that they and their families ate tref food. They desecrated prayer books and erased letters or words from mezuzahs and scrolls of the Law. There were even such evil-doers among them who lay with their wives before the latter went through their ablutions. They had affairs with gentile women and with married women.

A story reached Israel of a new false messiah, a sorcerer who preached conversion to Catholicism. In the German states, wealthy Jews had ceased speaking Yiddish, had become involved with Enlightenment, denied the Torah, devoted themselves to secular philosophy, to Latin and to other such worldly pursuits. Their wives went about bareheaded and in dresses that revealed their arms and parts of their breasts. Satan had, apparently, sensed that the coming of the Messiah was imminent, and he, along with his evil company of fiends and serpents, conspired to delay the redemption.

True, the rabbis tried to halt the epidemic of heresy and conversion, but when Israel took an accounting, in the dreary nights, of his own existence and that of the Jewish community of Okup and other places, he arrived at the conclusion that even the rabbis, the shepherds of the generation, were in error and sometimes inadvertently helped the Spirit of Evil. They had entered into excessive casuistry, into commentary for pure intellectual exercise, into scholarly ambition and had completely neglected the simple and honest Jew who yearned to serve the Almighty with sincerity and enthusiasm, not with hairsplitting. The rabbis themselves were isolated from one another, each engaged in his own subtilizing. There were many pious Jews who fasted every Monday and Thursday and observed various other fasts. There were penitents who, for the merest evil thought, went into exile. There were those who took a vow of silence for years out of fear of uttering a word of calumny and those who bound up their eyes to avoid looking at a female and lusting after her. But all this was linked with fear of punishment, and Israel contended that true service to God must bring with it joy and exultation, not depression and dread of Gehenna.

Israel took from the cabbala the expressions "the pettiness of thought" and "the greatness of thought." He who understands that the world is a part of God, His light, His wisdom, His mercy, doesn't tremble eternally in fear of the bed of nails. Serving God is to him a pleasure, not some obligation that must be paid. Israel realized something else: that the ordinary man couldn't outsmart and overcome the evil inclinations of the body all by himself. He needed a mentor to show him the way, to comfort and encourage him.

Israel didn't want to admit it to himself, but he sensed within himself the strength of a leader. In cheder, the boys had yearned to hear his stories. His fellow students at the yeshiva had confided in him, had told him all their secrets. Haskell, his wife and three daughters, who were already grown girls, were eager to please him and serve him. He often asked himself: "What do they see in me?" And he couldn't explain it. Oddly, even the peasant men and women of the village began coming to him to ask for his advice and his blessings. This was a mystery.

Something else occurred to Israel—he was able to read the minds of others. Even before a person could utter a word, Israel already knew what the other would say. Israel often had the feeling that he could ascertain from a person's face or even from his voice if he were true or false, humble or haughty, stingy or generous, as well as detect their worries and entanglements. Often he saw things in dreams that later came true; sometimes, these were trifles and even foolishnesses. Forces worked within him, and he didn't comprehend their meaning. The Evil Spirit and the Good Spirit waged a debate inside his brain, and he listened to their arguments as if he were a bystander.

The Evil Spirit often said that there was no God and that even if there was one, He was cruel to man and to beast. God had created them in such a way they would be in constant conflict with each other. Since He had created both the cat and the mouse, why had He instilled in the cat the urge to kill the mouse and sometimes, even, to torture it? How could an allegedly all-merciful father look on while Cossacks tore open the bellies of women and sewed hungry cats inside? What purpose did it serve for two bucks to butt each other to pieces for the possession of a doe? God is cruel, the Evil Spirit proclaimed, and those who speak of His benevolence are liars. The Evil Spirit pointed out many contradictions in the Torah. The same God Who said "Thou shalt not kill" and "Thou shalt not commit adultery" and "Thou shalt not covet thy neighbor's wife" condoned the raping of young women in war, murder and plunder. He even ordered the death of children. Well, and what about the sufferings of dumb creatures? How could ritual slaughter constitute a good deed? The Evil Spirit blasphemed God, and it sometimes took a long time before the Good Spirit found the proper words with which to answer him.

The Good Spirit countered that rage and enmity are only possible in those who feel wronged and who seek revenge. But how could the omnipotent God bear a grudge against His own creatures? How could a mother or a father wish to torture their own child? When a mother washes a child or anoints it with salve, the child assumes that the mother is doing it harm, while, in fact, she is doing it for its own well-being. The body is not the person, but only his garment, and a garment doesn't need to last forever. God's wisdom is available to anyone who has eyes to see. How can the wisdom of all the worlds and all the times be linked with evil? Why should the Divine Wisdom wish to torment an innocent child? Whoever acknowledges the wisdom of the Maker must also believe in His righteousness.

Sometimes, Israel grew weary of the constant disputes, and the best remedy he could find for this was a walk through the fields, gardens and woods along a path that led towards the Carpathian Mountains. The sky was clear blue and cloudless, stretching up without a barrier to endless heights. The sun exuded spun gold. Bees flew from flower to flower drinking in the nectar that they would later turn into honey. Huge birds soared in the heights, swaying on their wings like boats on a lake and emitting cries that delighted the ear and filled the heart with a faith that required no proof. The air was fresh and cool from the snow high on the mountains, blending the seasons of the year. Sometimes, in the middle of the day, the pale glimmer of the moon could be seen, combining night and day; yesterday, today and tomorrow. Israel recalled the passage in the Talmud to the effect that every blade of grass has an angel who stirs it, whispering: "Grow!" If a blade of grass has an angel to make it fulfill its mission, what of man, the crown of creation?

A stream ran through the forest near Grabica, possibly the same one that ran past Okup. The water here was even colder, but Israel immersed himself in it, swam, tried to tread water.

Here in the lap of nature, no cruelty was evident. The forest vibrated with song. Creatures chirped, whistled, twittered, buzzed and droned—each in its own fashion. Everything here proclaimed the presence of God, His grace and His splendor. Quite often, Israel took one or more books with him on his long walks. He would sit down on the stump of a felled tree and read about the Infinite One Whose light had filled eternity; about God's urge to create a world where His attributes would be revealed; about the World of Emanation; about the ten Sephirot; about the divine sparks that fell into the Abyss of the Great Female in the process of divine evolvement and that only a saint could extract with the force of exalted thoughts, virtuous deeds and holy names, thus hastening the redemption and putting an end to enmity, envy, anguish. The whole world, all the worlds, waited for the saint to redeem them.

Sometimes, in the evening, when Israel ate his supper with the family, Haskell, Haskell's wife, Dvosha, and his eldest daughter, Beila Basha, told stories, and Israel listened.

The village had a witch who healed the sick with herbs, with incantations and by pouring wax. The old woman was lame, her fingers were twisted and she could do no work, but a *lantuch,* a ghost, chopped firewood for her, brought water from the well, heated her stove, ground her grain in a hand mill.

A demon had taken possession of a village girl with six fingers on each hand and six toes on each foot. He had plaited her hair into elflocks. When she cooked, he tipped the tripod, soiled the food with devil's dung, spat and emptied his nose into the pots. Sundays, when she knelt in church, he inflated her belly like a drum. Sometimes he spoke out of her lips in rhyme, blasphemed God and Jesus and erupted into obscenities. The girl, a total orphan, had an old mare, and the demon also tormented this animal, braided its tail and rode it all night. After a while the horse died, and the girl was found drowned in the well—her head down and her feet up.

Haskell related that one time before Rosh Hashanah, on a night when the Jews in Okup recited penitential prayers, and he, Haskell, was getting ready to drive to town for the holiday, he came out of his house late in the evening to water a horse that had been grazing out in the pasture. Haskell had set the pail down for the horse to drink when, suddenly, he looked up in the sky. What he saw there astounded him so, that he felt as if rooted to the ground. Up in the sky floated a ship formed of light, with a similar make of sail. Haskell assumed that he was dreaming, and he pinched his own cheek. But it was no dream. The heavenly ship apparently floated swiftly, since in a matter of minutes it had reached the edge of the sky and vanished.

Haskell said: "I don't know till today what this was. How can a ship float in the sky? And why was it made of light? Maybe you know, Israel? After all, you study the sacred books. Is such a thing described there?"

"The world is full of amazing secrets."

"Were these angels or demons?" Haskell asked.

"Not demons," Israel replied.

"Maybe this was a ship of souls?" Haskell asked. "I say this because that summer there was an outbreak of cholera in Podolia, and it occurred to me that these were the souls of little children who had died in the outbreak."

"I don't know, Reb Haskell, I don't know," Israel said.

That night, Israel didn't fall asleep until the gray of dawn. Haskell did not have much Jewish education, but things had been revealed to him that weren't revealed to

rabbis or scholars. Israel recalled from the Gemara that during the time of the exodus from Egypt, a servant wench had seen visions at the Red Sea that hadn't been seen by the prophet Ezekiel. Sometimes things were revealed to ordinary men, women and children that the saints were denied the privilege of seeing.

The rabbis were wrong in holding ordinary Jews in contempt and in isolating women from Jewishness. To God, all Jews were esteemed. The soul of a contemporary male could have been—in a previous life—that of a female, and vice-versa. All the souls had been present on Mount Sinai. Children were certainly loved in Heaven. Jewishness had to be renewed, inspired with love and the glee of expectation. There was need of a leader to bring Jews together. In the Holy Land of old, the children of Israel gathered thrice a year in Jerusalem. True, we were then driven from the land, but in exile the law-abiding of the generation had to take the place of Jerusalem and lead the people.

Well, but how did one become a leader of the generation? For this, it wasn't enough to study the Torah and do good deeds. A man who hid couldn't become a leader. There had to come a time of exposure and communication. But how did the chosen man know that his time had come? And how could he know that he deserved to become a teacher of the generation? One could easily make the same mistake as Sabbatai Zvi. It was but one step from holiness to sacrilege.

Israel had heard the story of Joseph Della Reina, who had tried to summon the Messiah with holy utterances, but Samael, the arch-enemy, had muddled his thoughts and Joseph ended up uttering the wrong names and combining the wrong letters. Joseph had succeeded in capturing Satan, but he had given him a pinch of snuff, and this had been incense to the idols. Two sparks of unholy fire came out of Satan's nostrils, and Satan's chains fell down. Later, the same Joseph had become possessed by lecherous desires, and with his magic powers he lured into his bed the wife of the grand vizier and defiled himself with her. For a long time his soul didn't receive purification and wandered through wastelands and deserts, among demons and hobgoblins. It was reincarnated into snakes and dragons.

By the time Israel fell asleep, the sun was already rising, and he dreamed that he was in the Holy Land on a mountain near the city of Safad, in the Tent of Shalem. They were all assembled there—Rabbi Moses Alshich, Rabbi Isaac Luria, Rabbi Chaim Vital, Rabbi Joseph Caro and other saints and cabbalists dressed in white raiment. They were preparing to inaugurate the Sabbath. Their beards were damp from the ritual bath, their eyes glistened with love for the Queen Sabbath whose sanctity was so great that it surpassed that of the Messiah. The sun on the horizon filled the sky with gold and purple. Israel saw angels, seraphim, mansions, divine chariots, the Temple on High, the Holy of Holies.

A godly man in a prayer shawl and a white linen robe spoke to Israel and said: "My son, you and your deeds are known here. We listen to your thoughts and your supplications. You must remain in concealment for some time yet, but the day of your revelation is approaching. Be prepared, my son, to become a leader among the Jews. Fear not, for your intentions are pure. Saintly souls wait for you to show the renewed way to Jewishness. The patriarchs, the prophets, the men of the Great Synagogue, Tannaim and Amoraim, Gaonim and legists, the whole celestial family of ministering angels wait for you to correct what others have corrupted."

Israel awoke trembling. Usually dreams are forgotten. But he remembered this dream and all its details. Who was the old man who had spoken to him? Had he seen Elijah?

Israel made his ablutions and said his morning prayers. "What did I do to deserve such distinction?" he asked himself. He had only one answer—it was a merit due him because of his ancestors. He was descended from Jews who had perished on the pyres in martyrdom for God.

Since childhood he had yearned to elevate himself and others. Now he had awakened with a mixture of fear and exhilaration, as it is said in the Book of Psalms: "and rejoice with trembling."

He went out into the field to pray. Never before had the words of the prayers possessed such poignancy as today. Whoever is privileged to enjoy greatness of thought knows the gratification of praising the Almighty, of being united with Him. Everything comes from Him, after all—all beauty, all bliss. Even a worm in the ground enjoys His favors. Is it known, then, what a worm is? All the sages in the world could get together, and still they couldn't create a worm, a fly, a mite.

Israel prayed, and the stalks in the field and the trees in the forest prayed along with him. All creation prayed to God; everything He had made drew sustenance from Him. Those who try to deny Him or to estrange themselves from Him suffer the anguish of Gehenna even down here on Earth.

That morning, when Israel came back home, Haskell handed him a letter. Haskell had gone to Okup to buy salt, sunflower oil and axle grease, and a maid had given him a letter for Israel written in Hebrew mixed with Yiddish. Its author was Reb Shlomo Tereshpoler. Reb Shlomo wrote that Israel had worked a miracle. In saying goodbye before leaving for the hamlet, Israel had told Ittele that he hoped for the return of her father's inn. At that time, Reb Shlomo had wondered how he could ever get back his inn, for his competitor had already leased it from the squire for a period of five years. But this man had proven a swindler, and the squire had torn up the contract and leased the inn back to Reb Shlomo.

Reb Shlomo wrote that not only did he miss Israel, but so did his whole family. Abraham Gershon had already married the Kitewa Rabbi's daughter. Now it was Ittele's turn. Reb Shlomo explained that since Israel was an orphan and since he had no relatives to deal with a matchmaker, he, Reb Shlomo would ignore custom and himself propose a match to Israel. If Israel were willing, he should give up his teaching post and return to Okup, since Ittele was nearing seventeen. He was preferred by both the parents and the girl herself.

Israel could hardly believe his own eyes. All his wishes were coming true. But when things start going well for a person, he ought to take stock of his deeds. Often, the sinner gets all the good things in life and then, soon afterwards, comes the punishment in the other world; as it is written in the Book of Proverbs: "Pride goeth before destruction." A powerful wave of affection came over Israel towards Reb Shlomo, his son Abraham Gershon, his wife and his daughter Ittele—Israel's intended—that charming girl who for years had served him at the table and spoken words of solace to him. Now, this same Ittele would become his fiancee and, God willing, his wife and bear him children.

For a while, something within Israel grew tremulous from humility. What had he done to deserve this? And how would he be able to come near her? He both feared and wanted her; he was in awe of the union of their souls and terribly ashamed of the meeting of their bodies.

V

THE TIME both dragged slowly and raced along. Israel had read in a philosophical tract that time was a divine entity and therefore not to be conceived with reason. Well, but this is true of everything. Heaven and earth were like one huge cabbala volume full of mysteries upon mysteries. Every person and creature was a page from the Zohar, a line in *The Book of Creation*, a phrase from *The Tree of Life*. Even the prattle of a child had significance and contained allusions and homiletics. Many cabbalists had written in depth about a rooster's crowings. But just the same, the greatest of riddles appeared to be the passage of time.

One moment it seemed that Israel had just been in the village of Grabica and received the news that he would be betrothed to Ittele, and now that was all in the past—the engagement, the wedding. Ittele was already the mother of his daughter, Odel, named after Ittele's grandmother.

So many things had happened since Grabica! Reb Shlomo had at first prospered at the inn, and it seemed as though he would be able to provide Israel with board for many years so that he could study the Torah in peace and serve the Almighty. But for two years running there was a crop failure and an outbreak among the livestock. Horses and cattle suddenly took sick and gave up their breath. It didn't rain for so long that the stream in which Israel used to immerse himself years before went dry. Birds dropped dead out of the sky. Besides, Reb Shlomo's old competitor, the swindler, fabricated a false accusation against Reb Shlomo and informed the squire that Reb Shlomo had cheated him.

It was hard to believe that a Jew who knew the law could commit such an abomination, but human greed and the desire for revenge possess a black power. Even Moses had erred when he temporarily forgot his mission. Without a trial, the squire clapped Reb Shlomo in prison and ordered that he be given thirty lashes and fined fifty ducats. Reb Shlomo became ill and was left to starve. His wife, Israel's mother-in-law, grew sick as well, and Ittele was now carrying their second child.

Israel had to assume the task of earning a living. But what could one such as he do? He tried getting another teaching post, but, due to the crop failure and the drought, many fires had broken out in the Jewish towns, and there were now more teachers than pupils. No matter how much Israel looked, he wasn't able to land a position.

He had a strong urge to meet with Jews from other cities and towns and to hear their complaints against the world, against the rabbis, even against the Almighty. The rabbis and preachers constantly warned Jews not to complain against God, neither verbally nor even mentally, and they threatened them with the seven stages of Gehenna. But Israel felt that this wasn't always such a frightful sin. He recalled the saying in the Talmud that no man is punished for words expressed in a moment of anguish. The truth is that even Job the saint had—in his fashion—expressed resentment against Providence, and God didn't reprove him for this. It was one thing to have complaints and another to blaspheme. The rabbis in Poland tended to forget that man is flesh and blood, and there is a limit to what he can bear. The Gemara says that if Hananiah, Mishael and Azariah had been tortured, they would have served idols. Israel had no choice but to take to the road, and he evolved into a combination of preacher, advisor and comforter. In addition, he wrote amulets and gave sick people remedies that he found in the *Book of Raziel* and sometimes even in the Gemara and the Midrash.

The rabbis and most of the preachers avoided women for fear of being subjected to lascivious thoughts, but Israel received women and listened to their heartfelt words. Why did the rabbis tremble so in fear of Gehenna? Since everything was a part of God and His light, Gehenna too was part of His loving kindness. Israel had arrived at the conclusion that those who isolate themselves completely from their wives, who observe lengthy fasts, who constantly probe themselves for offenses against the divine law, who roll in snow in winter and in thorns and thistles in summer, are not reforming themselves. Many of them sink into dejection and surrender to complacency and haughtiness.

The rabbis and preachers often castigated Jews for drinking aquavit. They called any-one who had had a glass of spirits at a wedding or a circumcision feast a drunk. But Israel didn't agree with them on this either. The Psalms say that wine gladdens the heart of man. The prophet Isaiah predicted that when the Jews would return from exile to Zion, they would drink wine, be merry and sing. The sages of the Talmud mentioned that youths and maidens in the Holy Land had danced in the vineyards and thus had chosen their mates. Israel felt that many sins, such as calumny, theft, robbery, murder and lechery, stemmed from despair.

A number of rabbis and authors looked askance at Yiddish, considered it a language of women and know-nothings. True, the rabbis and scholars themselves employed Yiddish, for—since the destruction of the Temple—no one spoke Hebrew anymore. Hebrew mixed with Aramaic was used only to write books dealing with law, casuistry and morals. Jews who were scholars seldom consulted the Yiddish rendition of the Pentateuch or the storybooks written for women and common folk. But Israel loved the Yiddish language, and he even looked into the storybooks.

According to the Talmud, the angels listened only to Hebrew, but the Almighty knew all the languages. The Torah had been translated into seventy languages. It is said that before God gave the Torah to the Jews, he had first offered it to the descendants of Esau and of Ishmael.

Women came to young Israel to pour out their hearts to him. They bore their children in pain and in danger of their lives. Afterwards came the measles, the pox, scarlet fever, diphtheria and snatched the little ones back again. Those who were spared often went hungry. It happened more than once that a man disappeared, leaving his mate a permanently deserted wife.

The fate of the men wasn't much better. The priests incited against the Jews and asked that they be driven out of Poland as they had once been out of Spain. The mem-bers of the gentile craft guilds demanded all kinds of edicts against the Jewish artisans. From time to time, false accusations of ritual murders were fomented against Jews. A Christian child would get lost, and, right away, Jews were imprisoned and charged with murdering the child in order to drain its blood for their matzos. Frequently, Jews were broken on the rack and otherwise tortured until they "confessed" and were hanged. There never was a lack of witnesses who had allegedly seen the Jews seize the Christian child in a sack and drag it off to be slaughtered.

How could a merciful God allow all this and remain silent?

It wasn't easy for Israel to answer such questions. He pointed out that in comparison with God's wisdom, man's brain was less than a drop of water in an ocean, a grain of sand in a desert. Soon after their deaths, those Jews who died in martyrdom to God entered a higher sphere, next to which Earth with all its bounties and tribulations was less than nothing. He reminded those who listened to him that much of the suffering people endured they inflicted upon one another. How could man demand pity from the Almighty when he himself was cruel? Israel promised that the Messiah would soon come. There were many omens that the redemption was near and that the troubles that the Jews suffered were the birth pangs presaging the Messiah.

Those who came to Israel to decry their bitter lot always left cheered. The more affluent among them tried to shower him with presents, but he reminded his potential benefactors of the saying in the Book of Proverbs: "But he that hateth gifts shall live."

Israel himself was far from satisfied by the answers he provided for others. It was true that without suffering, without reward and punishment, man could not enjoy the greatest gift God had bestowed upon him: free choice. But how were the little children guilty? And why did the oxen, cows, horses and other animals have to suffer?

Sometimes Israel sank into what he called pettiness of thought. He was overcome with despair. He wanted to run off to some distant forest or even put an end to his life. Although he was no toper, God forbid, he took a glass of aquavit. He reminded himself again and again that all sadness issued from the Evil Spirit. He recalled the words he had heard from his father-in-law, Reb Shlomo Tereshpoler: "By moaning and whining, no one yet has built a house, plowed a field or sewn a garment." Man achieved everything with deeds, not by brooding. That held true in Jewishness as well. Sometimes at night, Israel was seized by a powerful longing for Ittele as well as a lust for her body. But more and more men and women came to listen to his words, to obtain his blessings, to tell him of their needs, and he could not leave them and go home. He might have been sad, but they were all cheered by his words. Their eyes lit up when he talked to them. When he left a town—mostly on foot—men, women and even children escorted him. Yeshiva students, young men boarding with their fathers-in-law left their wives and accompanied him on foot or by wagon.

Israel couldn't understand this. He spoke to everyone in simple terms. What he said could likely be grasped by a child of eight. He became famous, and he didn't know the reason why. Many people called him Israel the *Baal Shem* or Master of the Name. Others added the word "*Tov*," "Good."

Preachers began to grow envious of his popularity, and the complained that he was nothing more than a simple tutor and a near-ignoramus. O rs began to accuse him of playing up to the crowds and of flattering them. They labeled him a seducer and argued that he should be excommunicated.

Things happened quickly. Not only the common men and women, but also some rabbis and scholars came to hear him and chat with him. Among the rabbis there were those—mostly young men—who maintained, just like Israel, that Jewishness had grown too arid, too much involved in scholarly competition. The scholars themselves had lost the main essence: the love of Jewishness. They had seized everything for themselves—this world and the world to come—leaving no comfort for the common Jew. The rich men had all the say regarding the taxes that the Jews had to pay to the Polish crown; they frequently levied high taxes upon those who couldn't afford them and, at the same time, absolved themselves and their relatives or partners.

Among the Talmudic scholars who became Israel's disciples, or chasidim (as they had begun to be called), was his brother-in-law, Reb Abraham Gershon, who, following his father-in-law's demise, had become the Kitewa Rabbi. When Israel went to Kitewa to visit with his brother-in-law, he was received in the town not as some itinerant preacher, but as a man of renown. They called him a Zaddik—a man who is just, pious, virtuous. Respectable householders and community leaders came to Reb Abraham Gershon's house to welcome Israel. In the long conversations Israel had with his brother-in-law, he told him of his dreams, and Reb Abraham Gershon maintained that these were revelations from Heaven.

Reb Abraham Gershon felt that Okup wasn't the fitting place for Israel. The town was too small and too far from the Jewish centers. Besides, everyone there remembered Israel as a poor youth. How does the saying go? A prophet is without honor in his own town. Reb Abraham Gershon mentioned Medzhibozh. In comparison with Okup, Medzhibozh was a big city. There were more yeshivas there, studyhouses, inns for out-of-town visitors. It was already clear to both brothers-in-law that wherever Reb Israel settled, his adherents from Volhynia, from Podolia and from the far-off lands would gather.

In the two weeks that Israel spent in Kitewa, his path to Jewishness began to be ob-

vious to him, to his brother-in-law and to others as well. Israel didn't pray normally, but sang his prayers, each day in a different chant. The melodies came to him from nowhere else but the Mansion of Song. These weren't the cantillations of a cantor, but of one whose soul was both down here on Earth and in other worlds as well. That was how the Levites had sung in the Holy Temple. In his prayers Israel, as if complaining to the Almighty, waged with Him a discussion in song, and those who listened to him imagined that they heard the Almighty answer, defend Himself to Reb Israel, ask him to be patient and to have faith that what He did was all to the good.

Israel prayed according to the style of Rabbi Isaac Luria, and he often inserted into the prayers parts of the Zohar and sayings in Yiddish. The door to Reb Abraham Gershon's house was never still. Men, women, even children came, each with his or her own petition. Israel listened to everyone, and he tried to offer advice. Quite often, he uttered witticisms that evoked laughter.

An elderly man came to Reb Israel and told him that since he was on the verge of dying, he wanted Israel to recite his confession with him. The old man was yellow as wax. He supported himself on two canes. Those who had brought him had half-carried him inside. He was followed by his daughters and daughters-in-law, who lamented as if it were his funeral. Reb Abraham Gershon's wife, the rebbetzin, feared lest the old man die in her house. But the Baal Shem said to the old man: "How do you know that you are about to die? Did you make an agreement with the Angel of Death? Were you called up to judgment, and did you watch as you were erased from the Book of Life? How old are you, may the evil eye spare you?"

"Eighty."

"You call that old? At your age, Methuselah was still a boy. They first began offering him matches."

"Rabbi, what shall I do?"

"Have a glass of vodka, and let us drink to life."

Laughter broke out among the assembled. Those who had been crying just a moment before now laughed through tearful eyes. The old man himself smiled. The Baal Shem poured two glasses of aquavit, one for the old man and one for himself, and to everyone's amazement, the old man drank his down. He even chewed along on a cookie.

The Baal Shem told a paralytic to throw away his crutches, and he danced with him. He placed his hand on the foreheads of those suffering from headaches, and the pain soon left them. If the sufferer was a woman, he placed a kerchief between his hand and her brow.

Nothing like this had ever been seen by the people of Kitewa nor by those who had come there from other towns and cities. The Baal Shem himself tried to play down the miracles he had performed, but word of his approach to Jewishness and of his miracles spread. Every merchant, every pedlar carried his fame through inns, fairs, markets. Some of those who heard of his deeds suspected that a new Sabbatai Zvi had arisen in Poland; others promptly wanted to come see him.

Poland swarmed with those who probed the secrets of the cabbala, with wonder-workers, with men who had deserted their wives and children and had gone off to live lives of wandering and deprivation, with barren women waiting for miracle workers to unlock their wombs, with fund raisers from Jerusalem and from Safad, even with those who swore that they had come from the Lost Tribes of Israel on the other side of the Sambatyon, a river that hurled stones all week and rested only on the Sabbath. These Israelites claimed to be part of a nation that had continued to be free for two thousand years, had a king and mighty warriors, spoke the Holy Tongue and was isolated by deserts, high mountains and the miraculous river that protected them from enemies.

Poland still considered itself a great power, but the gentry were divided into all kinds of factions, and they could never come to any agreement in the Sejm, the parliament. Each squire had the rights of a Wojewoda, a governor. They waged suits among themselves that dragged on for years and ruined both litigants. Each of them could veto any law that went against his private interests. Everyone foresaw that, sooner or later, the Russians, the Prussians and possibly the Austrians would partition the land among themselves. Only a miracle could save Poland from disaster.

From time to time news reached the affluent Jews of Poland from such far-off lands as England, France and Italy; more frequently, they heard about recent happenings in the German states. A number of wealthy Jewish youths studied medicine in Padua and other universities, and when they came back, they told of telescopes that afforded views of the mountains and valleys of the moon, as well as newly discovered planets, comets and fixed stars. Astronomers had calculated with precision eclipses of the sun and of the moon. The Earth was round as a ball and inside it burned a fire that was spat out through volcanoes. When the sun went down, it didn't dip itself in the oceans but rose over America. There had evolved philosophers who denied that the Torah had been received from Heaven and that the Red Sea had parted at the time of the exodus from Egypt. They called the world "nature" and only recognized facts that could be ascertained with logic and with the senses. Israel the Baal Shem had heard of these unbelievers. One of them was an excommunicated Jew named Baruch Spinoza who denied God's power to perform miracles and tried to find contradictions in the Pentateuch and in the words of the prophets. He also maintained that all events are predetermined by the laws of nature and that good and evil are just human concepts or illusions—thus denying free will, reward and punishment and the existence of the soul.

VI

WHEN THE BAAL SHEM moved with his wife and two children, Odel and Eliezer, from Okup to Medzhibozh, he no longer had to wait for any sign for revelation. He had already revealed himself.

In the days and nights that the Baal Shem mused on his path to Jewishness, he concluded that even though God had given man the greatest gift of his treasure trove—free option—man was usually too weak to fully exercise this gift. Frequently, the ordinary person didn't know what to choose. The Evil Spirit often tried to persuade him that sin constituted a good deed, and vice-versa. The exercise of free choice required knowledge of every trick and wile of Satan, of all of his crafty devices. Jews could best garner joy by worshiping together, studying together, eating, drinking, singing and dancing together, and when they had a guide, a teacher, to show them the way. The teacher himself grew wiser in his strategy against the Evil Spirit when he listened to the people and learned the various temptations the Evil Spirit placed before each person.

In the brief time that the Baal Shem had been what he was, he had already encountered many passions whose extent he hadn't grasped until then, nor had he the skill required to overcome them. Men with beards and earlocks—fathers, grandfathers—lamented to Reb Israel that when they prayed or studied the Torah, they were assailed by erotic thoughts of loose women, of married women, of nude strumpets. Demons, imps, dybbuks whispered obscenities into their ears, composed smutty rhymes, cracked dirty jokes, even blasphemed.

A wealthy Jew, a philanthropist, admitted that he had been swindling his partner for years. He had repeatedly vowed to return the stolen funds, but he continued his offense. He awoke in the middle of the night, searched his soul and told himself for the umpteenth time that he was committing a crime; but the next day he did it again, as if against his own will.

A young man confessed to the Baal Shem that he had had intercourse with his young wife several times when she was menstruating. One disciple revealed that he was drawn to pederasty. In his dreams, he always copulated with men, even with his own brothers.

Some of the chasidim were men of wrath. The moment something occurred that went against their wishes or if someone said a word that displeased them, they fell into a rage, and it even happened that they responded with physical force. Frequently, these evil thoughts and passions assailed the men on the Sabbath, on holidays, even on the Day of Atonement. Just as the Jew stood reciting his confession and beating his breast in penitence, Satan pictured to him the joys of the flesh.

Many youths suffered from exaggerated fears of the tortures of Gehenna, from the urge to drop everything and flee to the ends of the earth or to hang themselves by their sashes. They found comfort only in the idea that there is no judge and there is no judgment.

One youth told the Baal Shem that while he sat and studied he could barely wait to hear the church bells ring. He thought of crosses, statues of Jesus, and a voice within him cried that Christ had been the true messiah and urged him to convert.

Each one came to the Baal Shem with his own idiosyncrasies or even madnesses. One young man had fasted to such excess that he was no longer able to eat. He kept on repenting for sins he had never committed or perhaps had committed in a previous life. When he rose to pray, he was overcome with tears and was unable to stop. His mother had told him that as a child he had inadvertently scalded his little sister with a pan of hot water, and she had died two years later of scarlet fever. It wouldn't have been his fault even if—God forbid—he had been the cause of her death. But he considered himself a murderer. He literally fasted from Sabbath to Sabbath. Winters, he rolled naked in the snow; summers, in thorns. He was so mortified by his illusionary sins that he no longer came to his wife even on those nights when she returned from her ablutions.

The men had their anxieties; the women, theirs. Those who were infertile could never come to terms with their barrenness. Why would God grant a woman a womb, ovaries and breasts if not to bear children? Somewhere there had to be a doctor, a conjurer, a leech or a sorcerer to help a barren woman. Some complained that the law was so written that the fault always seemed on the side of the woman. If a woman didn't give birth within ten years of the wedding, the husband was obliged to divorce her. But if a husband vanished somewhere and was never heard from again, the wife could never divorce and remarry. However, if once in a blue moon it happened that a wife left her husband or went insane or sank into a life of depravity, the husband was allowed to get a divorce by obtaining the signatures of a hundred rabbis.

A number of rabbis began to vilify the Baal Shem for receiving women. Women drove men to salacious thoughts. Listening to all the womanly gossip and babble, the rabbis said, went against the Torah. One of his disciples passed this opinion along to the Baal Shem, who countered jokingly: "So I'll settle for a smaller portion of the Leviathan. . . ."

Although the Jews in Poland and throughout the whole world heaped ever greater demands upon themselves when it came to the laws concerning kosher and tref, made a hundred laws out of each one, added to each paragraph in the *Shulhan Arukh* a whole dozen rites and restrictions that in later generations were transformed into new laws with more additions, some Jews often broke the laws dealing with the relations between man and man—the very ones that the Torah and the Prophets constantly warned them about. They slandered and maligned people. A number of merchants cheated in business, went bankrupt or were usurers. In many towns, the community leaders instigated against their rabbis and drove some of them out of town in disgrace.

The Baal Shem had repeatedly asked his disciples not to report to him the bad things the *misnagdim*, his adversaries, had uttered against him, but they constantly came to him with new gossip—this one had said this, that one had said that. In a number of towns in Volhynia and Podolia, arguments and even fights had broken out between Reb Israel's chasidim and the *misnagdim*. In several places, the enmity reached the degree that one side excommunicated the other, and the factions denounced each other to the gentry and the gentile courts—which was a desecration of God's law.

It happened that a chasid died, and the burial society refused to prepare the body for burial. The body then had to be buried beyond the fence, like that of some betrayer of Israel or a suicide. Just like the one-time followers of Sabbatai Zvi, the chasidim began

to form cliques, to do business with one another, to issue each other credit and to avoid merchants that belonged to the opposition.

When a rabbi died and a new one had to be chosen, both factions proposed their own candidates and cast aspersions upon the other side. There were moments when the Baal Shem deplored having become a leader among the Jews. "Who knows?" he mused. "Maybe my whole revelation was Satan's doing?" Well, but the good far outweighed the bad. Jews gathered from cities and towns, prayed together, sang, danced, grew enraptured. They didn't need to wait for a wedding, a circumcision or a redemption of the first-born to celebrate. Among the chasidim, each day was a cause for celebration. Delicate youths, seemingly pale and weak, were able to dance for hours without growing tired. At the same time, they chanted one passage or one sentence from the Gemara or from the Zohar again and again, hundreds or perhaps thousands of times, each time with renewed ardor. It was hard to gather where they mustered the strength for this.

Often the chasidim sang rhymes in Yiddish:

> *About the old one let us not ask after,*
> *Let us kick our legs as high as the rafter.*
> *Man of evil bent, may he repent.*
> *What was spoiled yesterday,*
> *Can be corrected today.*

By the term "old one," they meant the Evil Spirit, who, according to the midrashic interpretation, was an old fool.

The Baal Shem's son, Eliezer, was still too young to understand what was going on around him, but Odel was already four, and when she saw the chasidim dance, she would clap her hands and dance along. Sometimes the chasidim would draw her into their circle or someone would lift her onto his shoulders. Women from neighboring houses and even from near-by villages came to watch the chasidim dance and to clap their hands in accompaniment. Some brought cakes, cookies, cherry brandy. Some even brought along their children.

When the rabbis and the well-to-do householders heard what went on at the Baal Shem's house, they grew incensed. It was one thing to rejoice and dance with the scrolls of the Law on Simhat Torah; but to dance in the middle of the year was crazy. "I said of laughter: 'It is mad'; and of mirth: 'What does it accomplish?'" they quoted the words of Ecclesiastes. They pointed to the law that, ever since the destruction of the Temple, a Jew was obliged to behave like a mourner. Rumors spread that the chasidim drank to excess. Well, and why did women come to watch this evil? This was no religious festivity but an orgy, the *misnagdim* contended. There was but one remedy for this corruption: excommunication. The sect of chasidim had to be banished from the community, as had been the followers of Sabbatai Zvi and other semi- and total converts. There were some who demanded an assembly of rabbis from throughout Poland to excommunicate the chasidim with the blowing of the shofar and with black candles.

VII

FROM THE COUNTLESS REQUESTS for advice the Baal Shem received, he learned a lot not only about worldly affairs, but about Jewishness as well. The truth is that there is no difference between the two. Since everything comes from God and is a part of Him, how can one thing be called secular and another religious? Even a sin can't be completely severed from its divine sources. The company of Satan would turn to nothing if it severed itself completely from its celestial roots. Without light, what is darkness? If there is no life, what is the meaning of death?

The rabbis had one answer for all questions: kosher or tref, permitted or forbidden. But a Jewish leader was obliged to consider the total person with all his worries, needs, doubts, inclinations, aversions. Jews dealt with squires, many of whom were half-mad. Their bailiffs, stewards, bondsmen and relatives all had caprices with which the court Jews had to cope. From excess toil in the workshop, the kitchen, the store and from constant pregnancies and deliveries, Jewish women occasionally lost their minds, committed irrational acts, assumed unhealthy suspicions, often vented their bitterness upon their husbands, sons, daughters, daughters-in-law and sons-in-law.

Although the peasants had been slaves to the gentry for generations, they never ceased rebelling. Their prime victims often were the Jews who acted as middlemen between the landowners and their peasants and who were themselves half-slaves.

The summers in Poland were hot and often dry, and a day didn't go by that a Jewish town didn't burn down leaving the victims stripped of all their possessions. It also happened that the peasants would set fire to a landowner's palace. Although there was a saying that Casimir the First had found a wooden Poland upon his ascension to the throne and had left it built of brick and stone, this was merely a figure of speech. Most of the Polish castles, palaces and whatever they might be called were constructed of wood. Structures that had taken years or decades to erect were turned into ashes by a single spark. The same thing applied to churches, synagogues, stores and granaries.

God maintained His eternal silence, and the crushed spirits came to the Baal Shem to bewail their fate and to ask his advice. What to do? Where to go? How could one endure so much calamity?

The Baal Shem consoled the people, promised to pray for them, assured them that rescue was coming. Fire or no fire, God still ruled the world. How could mortal man conceive the ways of Providence? Even death wasn't the calamity people assumed. Suffering purifies man and broadens his outlook. The soul cannot be consumed by fire nor expire of starvation. The greatest trick during the worst of it, when the waters reach to the very throat and everything seems ominous, is to revive one's strength, praise the Almighty, pray with fervor, sing, dance and not lose one's confidence. After all, the past is already gone and tomorrow is yet to come. All that man possesses is the present. If you could introduce joy into the day, the hour, you would show Satan the back of your hand.

It happened more than once that those who came to whine and lament to the Baal Shem formed a circle and danced and sang and gave thanks to the Almighty for His mercy. Miracles occurred. Help came from unexpected sources. Jews wouldn't allow each other to perish. Neither did it serve the squires' cause to have their court Jews go begging. No one was safe from fire. Sometimes even a former enemy extended a helping hand.

The Jews in Poland had their own banks, which frequently consisted of the banker's breastpocket. A Jew wrote a letter in Lublin, and this letter was used to issue credit in Cracow, in Danzig, even in Leipzig. After all, grain grew in the fields, trees in the forests, fruit in the orchards. The rivers and lakes teemed with fish. Jewish brains found solutions.

At first, the Baal Shem downgraded his miracles. It had been God Who had helped, not he, Reb Israel. But in time, he himself came to realize that Heaven had endowed him with extraordinary powers. He would bless, and his blessings would come true,

sometimes virtually the minute he uttered the words. He encountered strangers, and before they even opened their mouths, he knew what they were about to say to him. When he prayed for someone, he often sensed his prayer being accepted according to the sign Rabbi Hanina ben Dosa gives in the Mishnah: "If my prayer is fluent in my mouth, I know that it is accepted; and if it is not fluent, I know that it is rejected." Occasionally when someone knocked on his door, the Baal Shem knew who it was going to be—a man or a woman—and what he or she would ask from him. Was it possible that he was privileged to be somehow linked to the Holy Spirit? But why and how? He was far from being a saint. Sometimes he was assailed by thoughts that were wild, even insane. Somewhere deep within his brain reposed a wag, a savage. He himself suffered from all the passions, anxieties and derangements he was supposed to cure in others.

He already had a large following, including rabbis renowned for their scholarship, and they hung on his every word and often interposed meanings into them that he himself didn't intend to convey. Sometimes he did things that were not precisely accepted practice. He frequently offered his morning prayers after the prescribed time. He couldn't address himself to the Almighty when his mind and his heart weren't ready. Sometimes he was not punctual with his evening prayers. The *misnagdim* attributed all kinds of minor sins to him, but the rabbis who were his followers constantly justified him. It often happened that a former enemy became an ardent adherent. When the Baal Shem ate with his disciples and left over a crust of bread, his followers broke it into crumbs which they distributed among themselves and swallowed. The Baal Shem told them that this was wrong. This was what the gentiles did with the wafers that the priests sanctified and represented as the flesh of Christ. But the chasidim contended that everything the Baal Shem touched became sacred.

His dreams grew ever more bizarre, more vivid, and he frequently recalled them in every detail when he awoke. He found himself in far-off cities, foreign lands. He sailed in ships across the sea. He wandered the streets of Rome, Athens, Persia. He traveled through Egypt. He saw Noah's Ark, the peak of Mount Ararat and the remnants of the Tower of Babel. Quite often, the Master of Dreams transported him to the Land of Israel, to Jerusalem, to Safad, to the Western Wall, to Rachel's Tomb, to the Cave of Machpelah. He talked to the Jews in those places in Hebrew and in Aramaic. He immersed himself in the ritual bath of Rabbi Isaac Luria. Not only people who were now alive, but also those who had lived in the past spent time with him, revealed the secrets of the Torah to him. He spoke with Rabbi Judah ha-Chasid, with Rabbi Chaim Vital, with Rabbi Joseph Caro, with prophets, Tannaim, Amoraim, Gaonim. He carried on conversations with Rabbi Meir the Miracle Worker, with Rabbi Hananiah ben Hakinai, and with such female saints as Deborah the prophetess, the matriarch Sarah, Queen Esther.

These were no longer ordinary dreams, but visions. Elijah the prophet came down to him in his fiery chariot and ascended with him to Heaven. He showed him all the seven heavens, all the worlds, spheres, temples. He heard the angels sing. So sweet were their voices, so exalted were their hymns, that he was left in a swoon.

The Baal Shem often heard it said that a man could only see things and people in dreams that he had seen while awake. What a lie! In dreams, the soul parted from the body, and whoever was so privileged could see marvels and treasures no living person had ever laid eyes on. Reb Israel awoke from these dreams with a sweet taste in his mouth, with the scent of incense in his nostrils and with the echoes of the celestial chants in his ears.

One night, he dreamed that Elijah took him to the mansion of the Messiah, called the Bird's Nest. The mansion was full of angels, seraphim, aralim, cherubim. They were all there—Adam, Noah, the patriarchs, the matriarchs, Moses, Aaron, King David, King Solomon, the prophets, Enoch, Metatron, Rabbi Simeon bar Yohai, Rabbi Isaac Luria, Rabbi Moses of Cordoba. The matriarch Rachel prostrated herself before the Throne of Glory and implored God to bring the Messiah, since the Jews could no longer endure all their persecutions and tribulations. Rachel warned that if things went on as they were, the world would be bereft of Jews, all creation would collapse, and God would be left all alone as He had been before the time of Genesis.

But Satan assembled his whole evil company and revived his accusations against the Jews. Satan argued that the Jews didn't deserve the Messiah. His demons and hobgoblins brought sackfuls of sins that Jews had committed: they chased after money, they swindled, they lent money at high interest, they gave false weight and false measure, they were meager in their charity, they put on airs, they molested their scholars and humiliated the poor. In the German states, the rich Jews had left the straight and narrow path to ape the ways of the gentiles; they adopted strange languages and took to reading secular books. It was the same way in other lands. The worst sin of the Jews,

Satan cried, was their jealousy, their enmity, which had brought about the destruction of the Temple.

The Messiah remarked to the Baal Shem: "Even more than the Jews want me to come, I want to come myself, but they themselves block my arrival."

The Baal Shem woke from the dream with a cry. His wife, Ittele, lying in the other bed, awoke too and asked: "Israel, what's wrong? Why did you cry out?"

It happened that Ittele was available for marital relations, having but recently attended the ritual bath, and the Baal Shem looked at her with love. Heaven had blessed him with a woman of valor. He had heard of wives who demanded luxuries, who wouldn't let their husbands serve the Almighty in peace, who yearned for costly furniture, jewelry, silk and velvet dresses and spacious houses. When their husbands brought an impoverished guest home, they greeted the guest with resentment, didn't give him enough to eat, declined to make up a bed for him and forced him to sleep in the poorhouse. Thank God, Ittele took his disciples and even strangers in need into the house, fed them, made up their beds, even did their wash. She had raised their children, Odel and Eliezer, to be helpful to the indigent. The awe of God reposed upon her lengthy face. The gentleness of a dove reflected from her eyes. Days passed by without him rightly hearing her voice.

He said to her now: "Don't worry, my beloved. I'm crying out of joy."

VIII

WHEN THE BAAL SHEM had first laid out his path towards Jewishness, he did it to guide a few individuals, not thousands or hundreds of thousands of people. He knew full well that each person must find his own road to God and that what was good for one man wasn't always good for another. Reb Israel still loved to go off by himself into the fields and forests. At these times, his wife worried and his disciples searched for him. There were those who believed that on the days and nights he was away from home, the Baal Shem ascended to Heaven. His disciples included a number of affluent men who tried to give the Baal Shem a carriage with horses and make him wealthy. But the Baal Shem continued to dress like an ordinary Jew, and when he left home to wander through the countryside, the peasants took him for one of the pedlars who came to buy up a bit of grain, chickens, eggs, honey or whatever they had to sell —often without the knowledge of the squire whose serfs they were.

The Baal Shem had a strong urge to settle in the Land of Israel where there still lived cabbalists who hoped to bring the Messiah through the power of holy incantations. Some of them lived in caves in the mountains around Jerusalem and Safad, and the Baal Shem wanted to become one of them. He often reminded himself that the duty of settling in the Land of Israel was incumbent upon every Jew in the world. True, the land lay in ruins, but the air of Israel was still imbued with godly wisdom. Often, emissaries from the Holy Land came to Poland to collect funds for its settlements and for the old men who had gone there so that they could be buried there when their time came. The

Baal Shem never tired of listening to stories about saintly Jews, pious women, graves of ancient saints, ruins of synagogues and studyhouses. In Jerusalem stood the sacred Western Wall, a remnant of the destroyed Temple. The Divine Presence hovered perpetually over the moss-covered stones. Even the gentiles in that land were different. They were the descendants of Ishmael, Esau, possibly of Lot—the children and nieces and nephews of Abraham. Their language resembled Hebrew and the language of the Targum—Aramaic.

It was rumored that the Baal Shem made several attempts to visit the Land of Israel, but he never got there. Many stories are told about these abortive efforts. Satan, Asmodeus and the other evil powers knew full well that if the Baal Shem ever reached the Land of Israel, he would surely bring about the redemption, and they determined to prevent this. One time, when the Baal Shem was about to depart, his wife fell gravely ill. Another time, it was his beloved daughter, Odel, who became sick. A third time, when the Baal Shem had already reached the sea, a terrible storm broke out, and the ship he was about to board sank. The Powers of Evil considered the Baal Shem their worst enemy, and they never ceased their war against him. They sent loose women to arouse sinful thoughts within him and to tempt him into adultery. Sorcerers of all types tried to lure him into desecrating the Sabbath, into eating forbidden foods, even into idolatry. When the Baal Shem went off to seek solitude in the forests, he was attacked by feral dogs, bears and snakes, and he had to drive them off with prayers and amulets.

The evil spirits and their female consorts had many wiles with which to entice a saint from the path of righteousness. The Baal Shem always outwitted them, but each time he was about to leave for the Land of Israel, they combined their strength to thwart him. The Messiah's time wasn't yet due.

Meanwhile, the years went by. Not so long ago, it seemed, the Baal Shem's children, Eliezer and Odel, had been little. Now, they were grown. Eliezer didn't turn out to be the man his father and his father's disciples would have preferred, but Odel, as it happened, had inherited her father's ardor, his love of people, his curiosity about the secrets of heaven and earth. At fourteen years of age matches were already being proposed for her, but Odel was choosy. She sought what in our time would be called "love." She had taught herself to peruse the sacred books. She listened to the teachings that her father dispensed to his disciples at the table, and even though his words were simple, she grasped their complexity.

Her mother was concerned that her daughter had grown unlike a girl was supposed to be—steeped in such female concerns as cooking, baking, knitting, darning, preparing to be a wife and to manage a household. But Odel apparently had the soul of a man. She went to the women's section of the synagogue and prayed not only on the Sabbath, like the other women and girls, but also daily, and chanted the prayers in tunes of her own composition like her father. She had taught herself Hebrew and had looked into the books of morals and even into the books of the cabbala. The women of the city said that when Odel married, she wouldn't be able to make a kugel for the Sabbath meal.

Ittele complained to her husband and begged him to urge the girl to behave like all the other Jewish daughters, but he countered: "She is my child and therefore can't be like the others."

"Israel, the girl is bringing shame and disgrace upon me."

"What's the disgrace? All the souls stood on Mount Sinai, the female too."

"Who will marry such a girl? She'll be left a spinster, God forbid."

"If the Angel has called out: 'Daughter of Israel be married to such and such,' he'll have to keep his word," the Baal Shem replied.

Still, he called his daughter to him to talk things over. The girl confided to her father that she couldn't be like the other girls. She couldn't even be friends with them. They thought only of cooking, eating, clothes, shoes. One wore her hair in one braid; another, in two. One wore a dress with pleats; another, with stripes. What difference did it make which garment enveloped the body? The men and boys studied the Torah, prayed with fervor and were immersed in Jewishness, and all that was left to the women and girls were pots and pans, clothes, diapers and swaddling clothes. She, Odel, couldn't lead such a narrow life. Odel had heard that Rashi's daughters had been Talmudic scholars. There had been female prophets among the Jews. In Spain and during Chmielnicki's time, the women had suffered martyrdom just like the men.

The Baal Shem didn't rightly know how to answer his daughter. He himself often mused on the fact that Heaven had somehow neglected the Jewish female, deprived her of the opportunity to perform a number of commandments, forbidden her to study the Torah. The women who bared their spirits to him often insinuated that they felt resentment against the men who had taken everything for themselves and left the women only the tasks of bearing and raising children, running households, preparing meals.

One evening, as the chasidim danced with particular enthusiasm, the door opened

and Odel appeared holding a kerchief in each hand. Normally men and women didn't dance together except at weddings, when the newly-married couple joined in the Virtue Dance. Even at those times, the bride and groom didn't touch hands but held the opposite corners of a kerchief.

When Odel appeared with the two kerchiefs, the chasidim grasped her intention—to be included in their circle, with a man clasping a corner of the kerchief on either side of her. For a while the chasidim were dumbfounded. But the fervor of the dance and the impact of the song were so strong in them that they drew her into their circle.

It just so happened that the Baal Shem wasn't present, but the women and girls who had gathered to watch the men dance emitted a collective shriek. Such a thing had never before been seen in a Jewish home, not even on Simhat Torah.

Ittele soon learned of her daughter's behavior and came racing all atwitter to plead with Odel not to dishonor her. But Odel didn't take any notice of her.

The chasidim now spun in a virtual whirlwind. Beards fluttered, eyes blazed. Someone ran to tell the Baal Shem what his daughter had done. He knew full well that if the *misnagdim* learned of this, there would be a terrible hue and cry. He was maligned as it was for receiving women's petitions.

The Baal Shem came to chastise his daughter for her improper conduct and to upbraid the chasidim for allowing her into their circle. But he paused in the doorway and for a long time didn't utter a word. This was no mere dance, he later said. This was how King David had leaped and cavorted before the holy ark. Legs soared with an ease that defied natural laws. The song erupted not from throats, but from souls. Never since the destruction of the Temple had Jews rejoiced this way. The circle opened once more, this time to admit the Baal Shem. The dance nullified all doubts within the brain; the song drowned out the last residues of sadness. The Gemara mentions that one can trust a gentile cook to observe the laws of Kashruth because a good craftsman would not make anything that would denigrate his craft, as would a cook's preparation of a mixture of meat and milk in a Jewish home. Could not the Divine Cook then be entrusted as well to do his work to perfection? The fire of faith consumed the thorns of envy, suspicion, hatred.

The women and girls who had been gazing at the dancing with rage grew so absorbed that their eyes gleamed. They clapped their hands and even sang along, knowing that when news of this reached the city, they would be denounced.

Ittele, the affronted mother, forgot the embarrassment her daughter had caused her. The Baal Shem had once said to her that even a sin committed with fervor was better than a good deed performed half-heartedly. He occasionally blurted out to her words that he later regretted, then pleaded with her not to repeat them to anyone, since the world was full of people who in the guise of piety were ready to harass others. They merely waited for someone to commit some error so that they could show off their scholarship and their adherence to the rigor of the law, to every petty restriction.

Even some of the chasidim had already been infiltrated by the wrath of those who were ready to root out their adversaries. The Evil Spirit had his adherents everywhere —in the marketplace, in the synagogue, in the studyhouse, in the burial society. Although Jews had for generations been themselves victims of false accusations and slander, there were those among them who had slandered and falsely accused geniuses, had made them resign their rabbinical positions, had even driven them from their towns in a wagon harnessed to oxen to increase their humiliation.

IX

THE YEARS PASSED, seemingly at an ever-quickening pace. Odel had found a young man she wanted for a husband, someone not from Poland or Volhynia, but from Germany, who had heard of the Baal Shem and had come to Medzhibozh to study under him. His name was Jechiel Michael. Jechiel Michael didn't speak a Polish Yiddish but a kind of Judeo-German. He had studied the Torah in the German city where he had been raised, and he lacked the quirks and gesticulations of the youths from Poland. Although among the Jews of Poland all marriages were arranged by matchmakers, and love in the usual sense of the word was considered an act of selfishness and promiscuity, Odel fell in love with Jechiel Michael.

She went to her father and said: "Father, don't be angry with me, but I've found my mate."

"Who is he?" the Baal Shem asked, and Odel replied: "Jechiel Michael, the one who is called 'The German.'"

The Baal Shem knew full well that his wife would disapprove of the match. The chasidim surreptitiously mocked Jechiel Michael. He studied the Gemara literally, without any casuistry. He was inclined neither to sing nor dance. He had blond earlocks, a reddish beard and blue eyes. He was fastidiously clean, polished his shoes, brushed his teeth every morning. He had brought along from Germany a book of travel accounts and another book with remedies for various ailments. These were all considered gentile ways. There were those among the chasidim who muttered that Jechiel Michael was a heretic. The Baal Shem himself looked somewhat askance at this strange disciple of his from a far-off land.

For a long while, neither the father nor the daughter spoke, then the Baal Shem said: "Daughter, I'll give you my decision tomorrow."

"Why not today?" Odel asked.

The Baal Shem replied: "I will consult Heaven."

The Baal Shem had never spoken this way before. His followers had already long claimed that the soul of their rabbi ascended each night to Heaven, but the Baal Shem had never personally admitted this. However, things had happened that no longer allowed any doubt. He performed one miracle after another. Nearly all his supplications were answered. When he took out a book to locate some passage, the pages turned on their own to the right place. Sometimes he even ascertained the sins one of his disciples was en route to commit, and the Baal Shem then warned him not to allow evil to overcome him. When one of his chasidim in a distant city fell ill or died, the Baal Shem already knew it before someone brought him the news.

The Baal Shem had read a book by Rabbi Joseph Caro in which Rabbi Joseph wrote about an angel who came to him each night, studied with him and pointed out to him the errors he had made or was to make. Now, the Baal Shem had such an angel too. The angel had not yet revealed his name or his face, but he spoke to the Baal Shem each night in his bed. He disclosed past reincarnations, not just Reb Israel's, but also his disciples'—Reb Dov Baer of Mezirech's and Reb Jacob Joseph of Polonnoye's, both Talmudic scholars. Saints as well as evil-doers came back to earth to correct errors they had committed in previous lives or to attain degrees of holiness they had not yet achieved.

When the Baal Shem told his daughter that he would consult Heaven, he was confident that his angel would come to him that night and give him an answer. And that's how it happened, or at least the Baal Shem felt that it did. Late at night when he had dozed off over *The Book of Creation*, a voice woke him. It was his angel's voice. He heard it say: "Yes, Israel, he is your daughter's destined mate. Both souls already await each other. Neither can go through purification until they have reached unity."

"Who were they in their previous lives?" the Baal Shem asked, and the angel mentioned the names of a male saint and a female saint who had lived centuries earlier. Due to some minor transgression they hadn't been able to have children, and they had

to return to Earth to become husband and wife again and to produce generations. Oddly enough, in that former life Odel had been the husband and Jechiel Michael, the wife. When the Baal Shem heard this, many things became clear to him about his daughter and about her intended as well. Something of the male had remained in Odel, and something of the female in Jechiel Michael. The Baal Shem had already known for a long time that many of a person's traits can be understood only by knowing of his former existence—who he or she was in a previous life.

The next day the articles of engagement between Jechiel Michael and Odel were signed, and a few months later the wedding was held. The Baal Shem had heard from the angel that a great saint, a leader of Israel would descend from this couple and that his name would be Nachman. The true heir of the Baal Shem would not be his son, Eliezer, but Odel's grandson.

We today know who this was: the great Rabbi Nachman of Bratslav, whose soul came down from the Throne of Glory and whose light had shone and would continue to shine until the end of generations. The Baal Shem did not commit his ideas to writing, but Rabbi Nachman left behind books whose depth and beauty have no equal. Like his great-grandfather, Rabbi Nachman yearned to go to the Land of Israel. He was privileged to achieve that which his great-grandfather did not, but only for a brief time and just shortly before his death. Again Satan intervened and obstructed the journey with many obstacles.

The Baal Shem had lit a great light among the Jews, but hardly enjoyed any personal satisfaction. He hadn't attained his goal—to bring about the Messiah. True, this wasn't Reb Israel's fault. But at night when he lay awake, he often reproved himself that it was because of his shortcomings. The Baal Shem had wanted chasidism to uplift the common Jew, considered an ignoramus, and to improve the lot of the common Jewess as well. But as time went by, the rabbis and scholars took over chasidism. A number of affluent, even rich men began to gravitate towards the movement. When a crowd of Jews came to the Baal Shem for the Sabbath or a holiday, the wardens seated the wealthy and scholarly along the eastern wall, and the paupers were left to stand by the western wall. Again and again the Baal Shem admonished his men that this practice went against his will, but he couldn't bring himself to enter into a feud with them or dismiss them, since they earned their livelihoods in this fashion.

His disciples began to involve themselves in the communal affairs of their local cities and towns and to see to it that the posts of rabbi and ritual slaughterer went to fellow chasidim. Cliques formed even in the Baal Shem's house of prayer. Some wanted Reb Dov Baer to take over after the Baal Shem's demise, others opted for Reb Jacob Joseph of Polonnoye. The Baal Shem's son, Reb Eliezer, had his own little group of supporters.

There were days when the Baal Shem wanted to doff his silk gabardine, don a cotton jacket and a sheepskin hat, sling a sack over his shoulders and go out to a life of privation—become a woodcutter or a water-carrier. But when he started talking about this, Ittele would burst into tears. He no longer had the strength to walk great distances or to do heavy labor. He suffered stomach trouble. He couldn't dance for so long or with such intensity as before. Although the Baal Shem constantly brought up the fact that Jews must be joyous, he could not free himself from sadness. He had listened to so much Jewish misery that he could no longer feel as confident as before. One time it was a blood accusation against Jews in some city, the next time in another place. Epidemics broke out, fires. Every squire issued different decrees against the Jews. The priests didn't cease reminding their flocks that the Jews had murdered God's son, for which they were to be condemned forever.

The plague of heresy grew stronger with time. Many scholars and philosophers preached that man could trust only his senses and his reason. Others declared that not even one's reason could be trusted and that what one saw with one's eyes was merely a dream. The Baal Shem had one source of consolation—that all these were the birth pangs preceding the coming of the Messiah. Long, long ago, the Mishnah had predicted that "With the footprints of the Messiah presumption shall increase and dearth reach its height. The vine shall yield its fruit, but the wine shall be costly; and the empire shall fall into heresy and there shall be none to utter reproof. The council-chamber shall be given to fornication. . . . The wisdom of the Scribes shall become insipid. Children shall shame the elders, and elders shall rise up before the children, *for the son dishonoreth the father, the daughter riseth up against her mother, the daughter-in-law against her mother-in-law; a man's enemies are the men of his own house.* The face of this generation is as the face of a dog." Everything the Baal Shem heard gave proof that this time was coming not only among the gentiles, but among the Jews as well. One of the Amoraim had said that if the Messiah were to come, he, the Amorite, didn't want to be alive to see him. The Baal Shem sometimes thought the same about himself.

At times he felt a weariness with the material world and its pitfalls. He hadn't the

strength to endure the war between Gog and Magog and all the other troubles looming like a black cloud over the world. A dark foreboding drifted towards the Baal Shem from the Turkish lands. A new Sabbatai Zvi by the name of Jacob Frank had arisen, one who was a sorcerer, a lecher, a seducer. He already had a following in Poland.

The one comfort for all these troubles was freedom of choice. Man still had the power to choose between good and evil, sanctity and impurity, between the licentiousness that stems from resignation and the joy that arises from the realization that in the final analysis everything must emerge for the best since God is all mercy and no evil can come out of mercy. No soul can be repudiated forever. A great light had to come down upon the world along with a divine joy brought about by the Jew and his Torah.